SHOW YOURSELF A MAN

POWER PRINCIPLES FOR MANHOOD

Anthony Simmons

Diligence Publishing Company
Bloomfield, New Jersey

The Scripture in this book is from the King James Version and the New International Version.

SHOW YOURSELF A MAN

Power Principles For Manhood

To contact Anthony Simmons to preach or speak at your church, organization, seminar, or conference email: powerintheword1@yahoo.com

SHOW YOURSELF A MAN

Power Principles For Manhood

ISBN: 979-8-9869173-4-4

Printed in the United States

TABLE OF CONTENTS

DEDICATION

This book is dedicated to all of the men out there holding it down in the best way they know how. Always remember that yesterday is gone. Today is a brand new day, and you can start over again. Keep fighting my brother. Your battle will end with you coming out on the winning side.

Also, I personally dedicate this book to the following men:
My spiritual leader, Apostle Ron Toliver, the other spiritual leaders who have poured into my life, Apostle Matthew Tillery, and Bishop Dr. Donald Hilliard Jr., to my sons, Justin Simmons and Marcus Simmons, to my brothers, Larry McCrea, Rodney Simmons, Michael Simmons, Louis Simmons, Gary Thomas, and Derrick Bouie, and to the memory of my brother Greg Carter, to my Grandsons, Joshua Edmund and Haneef James, and my great grandson, Ezarie.

When David's time to die drew near, he commanded Solomon his son, saying, "I am about to go the way of all the earth. Be strong, and show yourself a man.
(1 Kings 2:1-2)

CHAPTER 1

THE CURSE IS BROKEN

Far too many Broken Men have produced far too many Broken Homes, but Christ came to break and to put an end to this negative and downward vicious cycle that has been disabling families from becoming their best and reaching their full potential. Christ confessed that He came to open our spiritual eyes and understanding, to heal our hurts, and to break us out of bondages and spiritual blindness (Luke 4).

So many men never see how much suffering they cause to others and how much pain they produce in people that they love and care about. These evil and unproductive cycles must come to an end. God created men to be leaders by example of real and authentic discipleship. Man's divine position in the family is the head. We have been called to be the Priests, Providers, and Protectors of our families (Ephesians 5:23). The headship of the man has been clearly spelled out in the Bible.

Christ is the Head of the family, and as men submit to His ways, then their responsibility will gain respect from their wives and children. The Bible never said we were the boss of anyone. It said take dominion over animals, birds, fish, and the Earth, not over our loved ones (Genesis 1:26). As men we should be fruitful, multiply, and increase good traits and things that will bring God glory and not grief.

The world system has lied to and deceived many men because of their pride, ego, and stubbornness to rule by force and not by faith in God's Word. As men, many times our prayers are going unanswered, and our kids are carrying around in their lives unresolved anger, low-self-esteem, low self-value and low-self-image because of our ungodly behavior and decisions. Although I hesitate and hate to admit this fact and reality because of who I am today and what God has allowed me to achieve and to accomplish, I spent many wasted years being a "curse" unto my family instead of a "blessing."

The Bible has a name for this kind of dysfunction – the "curse." In the Bible, the curse is when God hands people over to the consequences of seizing blessing on their own terms. It is a curse because, instead of abundance and life, we end up with scarcity, isolation, and death. A curse is also when there is a call for punishment, harm, or injury to come to someone.

Unresolved anger is a big and repeated recycled reason why so many men cannot "show themselves to be men" who are effective, impactful, satisfied, and complete. We put our families at such a disadvantage when we do not deal with our past issues. Many of us men have never treated or received therapy for those experiences in life that have shaped and formed our way of thinking. We hide behind fear of failure, insecurities, violence, abuse, addictions, alcoholism, and even irresponsibility. Many become controlling, narcissistic, abusive, reckless, criminals, and even players with the lack of ability and capacity to commit and to become dedicated, loyal, and faithful to our families and the women in our lives.

Men we desperately need God's help to change most of our ungodly conditions. We need to become men who have godly character, commitment, competence, capacity, and courage.

Many of us men indirectly take out our frustrations on our families. In 1990 when I lost my first-born daughter to a rare congenital heart disease at 6 days of age, I became very angry and tremendously depressed for a very long time. This negative mindset of mine messed up many of my relationships and created in me a hostility that I did not know how to deal with. But my faith in God and His Word healed me and made me whole again. No parent should ever have to outlive their child or bury their child. They are supposed to be the ones burying us as parents. But once I was healed, this very painful part of my past produced and developed in me an attitude of gratitude for the things still alive and that are working in my life. It changed my thinking and attitude towards my opportunities and those that I love and care about. Since then, God has giving me a since of restoration by blessing me with another daughter that I adore tremendously through my second marriage. He turned my pain into pleasure and my curse into a blessing.

Men, the God of endless Grace and Mercy is giving us opportunities to turn our lives around, and to get our houses into Godly order. Let's stop wasting time, energy, and resources on sexual immorality and things that are destroying us instead of building us. "Manhood" is a level of Maturity and Responsibility that is needed for us to become the Men and Leaders that we were born to become. Men, we can turn "negative" beginnings into "positive" endings if and when we begin to do life God's Way.

1 Corinthians 13:11 When I was a child, I spoke as a child, I understood as a child I thought as a child, but when I became a Man, I put away childish things.

Through my sinful actions, I was creating unhealthy relationships within the family, unknowingly developing financial hardships and lack of money issues, causing suffering, sicknesses, and diseases by opening the door of destruction and dysfunction to unintentionally enter into my home and my household, bringing negative emotions and bad feelings, vibes, and energy among my loved ones, unleashing unforgiveness and uprooting peace, power, harmony, and unity, and allowing ungodly, sinful, and unproductive characteristics to be within my family bloodline. But God began to change my character from a liar and a deceiver into a true man of integrity. He gave me a greater capacity to carry more responsibility. And God began to give me a desire for increased competence to gain the knowledge I needed to become a better man and a greater leader. He is truly a God full of Grace and Mercy and unlimited opportunities and possibilities to get our lives together and to get our houses in order.

These positive changes that we need as men are all possible through the Word of God, the Bible. The Word of God explains to us how we all have a treasure of unlimited gifts on the inside of us, but the devil – the thief, who steals, kills, and destroys our potential and possibilities, has blinded the minds and thoughts of countless men that do not believe or who cannot see nor receive this Truth. You shall know the Truth (Jesus), and the Truth (Jesus), will make and set you free. Unfortunately, so many men are stuck in bondage and cursed conditions.

Faith is produced by hearing God's Word and this is why many men are limited spiritually from becoming successful in every area of life. So many choose not to come to church and Bible Study, nor attend corporate prayer. People are perishing for their lack of knowledge and understanding. No Vision, no Victory, because where there is no vision the people perish. Many cannot even imagine a better life for themselves and their families because they repeatedly refuse to do life God's way. Jesus followers were called disciples because they willfully and voluntarily learned new and different godly ways and principles of discipline and self-control. My ways are higher than your ways and my thoughts are higher than your thoughts, says the Lord God Almighty. Jesus said apart from Him we can do nothing worthwhile, but with Him we can do all things. This is why I love this challenge that King David is giving to his son Solomon who will be his successor over God's people.

King David is about to die, and he has a talk with his son Solomon about how to remain in a place and position of God's power, promises and prosperity. He challenges and charges Solomon to stay in the will of God by obeying His commands and living according to the principles that are written in the Bible. David tells Solomon that if he was to walk in the ways of God by keeping His laws, regulations, and decrees, God will always make a way for him to sit in a position of power and authority as King on the throne. David told his son to be strong and courageous and to "Show himself a Man" or to prove his manhood by becoming responsible, reliable, and accountable to God in every area of life. I believe that God is challenging men today the same way, to become positive and not destructive leaders of their

13

families. I really commend and applaud all fathers who take the time to advise any of their children on how they can have a better quality of life. Fathers who take the time to teach, train, and demonstrate positive principles that are powerful and effective towards a productive and fulfilled life. David was told by God that if his descendants live as they should and faithfully follow Him with all of their heart, soul, mind, and strength they will always rule and reign over His creation and have success in every area of life.

Be fruitful, multiply, and occupy until I return, is what God commanded man after making man in His Image and likeness and Blessing and anointing them with supernatural ability (Genesis 1:28). This is a pronouncement and description of a generational blessing from God, but unfortunately far too many men are not doing what is required of God and are in actuality living under a generational curse.

How in the world can we "show ourselves as men" when so many of us were never taught or have ever seen an example of real manhood? Manhood must be taught and learned, and not assumed that it will automatically happen. The culture and the world's definition of manhood and fatherhood is drastically different from God's and the Bible's teachings and beliefs. We as men have to avail ourselves to scriptural truths as it relates to what God wants and expects from us as men and as being the head of our households. I believe that we are living in a time, age, and era where we as men need more than ever that fathering spirit of the Apostle Paul that was so beneficial and instrumental in the development of his spiritual son Timothy. Paul said there will be many teachers but not too many fathers. He told Timothy that his mother Eunice and his grandmother Lois had great faith that they had passed onto him. Paul followed saying to Timothy, "Stir up and develop this faith and your gifts by my laying hands on you and by me praying for you."

We desperately need men who have faith in God and men who know how to pray. I believe Timothy like so many men in our day was intimidated and controlled by fear. But Paul reminded him that that spirit is not from God, but from the enemy. God gives us the Spirit of love, power, and a sound mind so that we can provide for and protect our families. Men, we more than ever before need to be led by our faith and not our feelings. To lead by example, and to process and manage effectively our emotions of pride, lust, anger, disappointments, and our thinking. We must become transformed by the renewing of our minds (Romans 12:1-2). David was constantly overlooked by his own father Jesse, who obviously did not realize the qualities and abilities his son possessed and developed. After Samuel poured anointed oil on David to become King, the bible says that God's Spirit was on David's life from that point on. Coming from the world into the Church at age 30, I can testify to you that God's transforming power through the Holy Spirit is powerful and real. It's time to make positive changes in our lives, and it is time to denounce and depart from negative actions. God the Father loved God the Son in the person of Jesus the Christ. So much so that Jesus said I do nothing without my Heavenly Father instructing me first.

So many men such as myself were taught all the wrong principles and patterns of "Real Manhood." I was raised in a single parent household by my mother who did the best she could by raising me and my seven siblings. I grew up in the city of Newark, New Jersey where I often saw pain, poverty, problems, and violence. As a result, I had a few encounters with the police as a teenager and young adult, but because I had a praying mother, I never got that first felony that would ultimately limit and destroy some of the opportunities I have had towards a better life.

I remember being stopped for driving while intoxicated. I had no car insurance and a failed inspection sticker. They did not tow my car and when I went to court, the judge gave me a small fine. Once my friend and I were illegally selling marijuana and got caught by the police. As they were driving us to the precinct to arrest us, they suddenly stopped the car and set us free with no explanation. Another incident I was pulled over and hand cuffed in front of my wife at the time and son, and they took me to a holding cell and gave me a court date. While I sat and watched many people having their driver's license suspended or revoked, I prayed for favor. I surely would lose my job and dignity. But again, the judge gave me grace and a scolding. My mother's prayers helped me get out of trouble a lot.

I do not recall, being the youngest in my family, my father ever living with us or any other interactions with my mother or siblings. Research and studies have shown that 57% of Blacks, 33% of Hispanic, and 27% of Whites have no biological father in the home. How can the blind lead the blind? The Bible asks. Will they both not fall into a ditch? My brothers and I started off in a deep, despairing hole with a deep dark deficit as it related to manhood or becoming a man. My older brothers, with me being the youngest, gave me my only early examples of manhood. That consisted of drinking, getting high, partying, and women, to which I followed suit. They did work but struggled maintaining employment because statistics show that sons who grow up without their fathers have difficulty obeying authority. They tried their best to teach me how to fight and defend myself physically, how to avoid dangerous and life-threatening environments and situations, and also how to work and earn wages to make a living. But although they did their best to pour into me what they never had poured into them, I was still left with that fatherless wound, injury, and brokenness.

The Word of God says there is nothing new under the Sun, and as I observe the illnesses and spiritual sickness of our society and culture, only God can change and convert this negative narrative of a "Fatherless Generation." Almost 39% of children growing up today are coming up in a single parent household. This reality creates so many long lasting negative and damaging challenges for kids. These children are more likely to live in poverty, have low self-esteem, drop out of school, struggle with addictions, and develop identity crisis. They also tend to have abusive relationships, anxiety disorders, chaotic lifestyles, and are more likely to commit crimes. On the other hand, when that father is present to lay down the laws of the house and enforce them, those children are twice as likely to go to college, 80% less likely to go to prison, and in many cases avoid teenage pregnancies.

God says, if my people who are Called by my name would: 1. Humble themselves 2. Pray 3. Change their evil ways first 4. Seek and Search for Me with all their hearts and effort. Then and only then will I begin to heal the World and fix the broken parts of people's lives (2chronicles7:14).

We can reverse the curse! I believe that we have a real chance of a Holy Ghost revival that will radically change our world for the better. A revival where people would turn back to God and leave idolatry behavior. We must get back to our "First Love" and put God as a priority over everything and over everyone (Revelation3).

In my first marriage, oftentimes I behaved and acted like I was still single, it was learned behavior. When we know better, we are expected to do better. Today, I'm in my second and final marriage of over 25 years. I have learned the value of functioning families that minimizes dramatic and destructive behaviors. But you cannot live what you do not know. As a result of my dishonoring and mishandling that first marriage, it ended in divorce and put a serious breach and communication gap between me and my two sons. I was creating for my sons what was done to me by my father. Neglect, absence, and financial mismanagement of money.

We as men do not realize the hurt, harm, and devastation our actions bring into the lives of our children that stirs up so much anger and resentment within them and can sometimes develop into hate towards us as men. I have since resolved and repaired those relationships with my sons through apologies, communication, my actions, and unconditional love. I still have hope because I have met some men who realize the error of their ways as well and have attempted to reconcile their relationships with their children.

Note: To all Ex-Wives and Ex Girlfriends who hate their Ex-Husbands and Ex Boyfriends justifiably so! Please do not prevent that man from having an opportunity of an ongoing and healthy relationship with that child or with their children. Do not use your hurt to hurt them at

your child's expense. We cannot deny that longing and endless desire that our children have for the missing biological parent. You will not regret it in the long run.

CHAPTER 2

MAN UP

Another way that we as men can "show ourselves to be men" is by showing up. It`s Time to MAN UP! Oxford dictionary meaning of the phrase "Man Up" is defined as for a man to be brave, courageous, and tough enough to deal with difficult or unpleasant situations. To demonstrate toughness, strength, and ability. In sports man to man defense means to defend a specific player by yourself without any help from others. In football when a particular cornerback or safety defends or covers a particular wide receiver or tight end, that is considered man to man defense and coaches would yell, it's time to "man up," implying that it is that player's sole responsibility to guard his opposing player. Likewise, in basketball, to minimize an opposing team's best scoring player, the coach would attempt to prevent that player from scoring by putting their best defensive player on him and would say, "man up," no more zone defense. So it is the same way in life brothers. God wants men to take care of their responsibilities and simply "Man Up." No more excuses of why we can't! No more reasons of why we are missing in action. And no more lies on why we are not doing what we are supposed to be doing. These are 7 ways in which we can "Man Up."

1. **Show Up.** Your presence and participation in your family affairs makes a huge positive impact on their self-value, identity, personality, self-esteem, and their joy and fulfillment. When you carve the turkey at Thanksgiving dinner and pray over the family, it makes everyone feel more protected, provided for, and important. When men show up there to lead by example, everyone begins to understand their roles and place in the family. When you show up at the game to cheer them on, it does something amazing to them mentally that cannot be explained, because they simply want to make you proud of them. And when you show up to special occasions and school events like plays and back to school night and PTA meetings, it

makes them feel proud and loved and accepted by you as well. Even when you spend quality time with the family at cookouts, recreational amusement parks, going shopping, or simply watching movies and TV together, it makes a world of difference to everyone. Also going to Church as a family, worshipping together, praying together, Sunday dinners together, drastically increases the spiritual strength of all.

2. **Step Up.** When I was a teenager, my mother remarried my stepfather who willfully stepped into my absent father's position as provider and protector. He accepted the role of helping my mother to raise her eight kids who were not his biological children, but nonetheless, he loved all of us and treated us as if we were his own. Likewise, my wife helped me to raise my two sons from my first marriage and stepped in and became a mother to them like they were her own and loved them unconditionally. I also stepped in and became a father to my wife's daughter from a previous relationship who is not my

biological daughter, yet I love her as though she is. Sometimes brothers, we have to step into situations where there is a need and fulfill the voids and repair the damage left by others. In the movie "Claudine," James Earl Jones, who was a garbage man and Diane Carrol, who was a single mother on welfare, portrayed a couple who struggled against the governmental structure and systems that were used to keep people of color oppressed and in poverty. But they decided to risk financial security and convenience for the greater good – their love for each other. Sometimes we will be asked to take the hard and not the easy road. Step up to these difficult roles and duties because you have been chosen to do so.

3. **Grow Up.** Act your age! Maturity is a real challenge for so many men. Xbox, Play Station video games, sports, and the lack of understanding real manhood, keeps many men ineffective, dysfunctional, and broken. Not willing and not being able to recognize and to obey authority leads to many men not being able to keep a job and thereby unable to provide financially for their

families. Immaturity also leads to criminal activity not realizing the devastating consequences of a felony long term. It closes so many doors of opportunity for a better quality of life, and it puts limits and restrictions on your upward movement. I often witness grown men who still live at home or with girlfriends who these men depend on to pay most of the bills and carry most of the responsibilities of the household needs. Brothers it's time to become aware of our roles, goals, and expectations. Our families need us to handle car repairs, maintenance problems, cut the grass, shovel the snow, go to work, and protect them from evil intended people that are ready to exploit their weaknesses and take advantage of their lack of covering. When I was younger, I just wanted to party and have fun and watch TV and be lazy all of the time. But when I was taught better, I began to do and behave better. Some believe that if they are above the age of 18 or 21 that they are automatically a grown man. Age is only a number that allows you to legally drink, and to legally drive, and to do other adult things. But when it comes to God, you must demonstrate that you are a man.

4. **Go Up.** We must occupy and multiply while we have time and ability to do so (Genesis 1:28). God has blessed you to become a blessing just like Father Abraham. Your Time, Your Talents, and Your Treasures belong to God. He has Gifted you with greatness so that you can become great. You have been born with natural skills and abilities to become successful in every area of life. You must get Victory over every battle that you will encounter. Pray like Jabez did and ask God to enlarge your territory and to expand your borders (1 Chronicles 4:10). God has given you the ability to get wealth (Deuteronomy 8:18). The sitcom "The Jeffersons" was a funny and entertaining show about George Jefferson starting a dry cleaner's business that grew and multiplied into many other successful stores. The song *Moving On Up* was so inspiring and motivating to viewers who thought of the possibilities of going from rags to riches. My wife, who went from welfare to Wall Street, made a huge and

significant increase in her income, because she was determined to go higher. Brothers, let's get a plan of action by investing, saving, budgeting, giving, and making money. If you fail to plan you plan on failing. Go to God for a strategy to get out of debt and/or poverty!

5. **Push Up.** Pushups as a form of exercise gives our arms, chest, shoulders, and backs strength and definition. The resistance and energy it takes to do pushups in the natural is very exhausting and depleting to our muscles and nervous system. By the same token, there are times that others are looking to us to push them into their purposes. Possibly as a mentor or coach, you can encourage and empower others to achieve and accomplish their own personal dreams, goals, and aspirations. We all at times need invisible hands in our backs to push us into our prosperity. This will take an intentional effort and sacrifice from you to serve others as you continue to pursue and work on your own mission. Become a good steward of what God has entrusted you with. The two greatest

commandments tell us to love God and to love our neighbors as we love ourselves, and the Bible teaches us to esteem others higher than ourselves. Men, this can be tiresome to over extend yourselves for the sake of others. But please share your resources with others that will push them into their destiny. Your rewards will ultimately come from God and not from man. As you detect, see, observe, and assess the potential and possibilities in others, you as a mentor or coach can help them discover and perfect life changing skills and attributes short and long term.

6. **Pull Up.** Failure is not a person, but it is an event. Yesterday ended last night but today is the first day of the rest of our lives (Zig Ziglar). God is a God of grace and mercy, and a God who forgives us. I have had so many second chances in life that I have lost count. Many seasons of being down and feeling like a loser and a failure. But I can recall in each low and down season in my life, God would send people periodically to pull me up. We are all called to lift, love, and liberate others. The Bible says forget

the former things because God is doing a new thing. The Apostle Paul talked about how he was determined to forget those things which are behind him and to press towards the future. It's very hard at times to shake ourselves free from suffering or feeling sorry for ourselves with pity. This is why at times we must pull people out of their despair who do not have the desire or strength to do so themselves. During my 2-year battle against stage 2 colon cancer, God used many to pull me up when I felt like staying down. All my doctors were professional yet occasionally very personal and went out of their way to spend time with me when things went wrong. It was so encouraging to me in those moments that they would interrupt their rounds just for me. My wife was my biggest inspiration and hand up when I needed it the most. Her prayers, daily visits, and love for me was demonstrated when I was down. My Church, family and friends all showed up when I needed to be pulled up. You never know the value of a visit, the care of a call, the timing of a text, or the power of a prayer, when someone is in need of a pull.

Just like a disabled car needs a tow, discouraged and disappointed people need a spiritual tow also. The Word says we have to snatch some out of the fire, just like firemen run into a burning building to save others.

7. **Look Up.** I will look unto the hills from whence cometh my help, my help comes from the Lord (Psalm 121). Jesus said apart from me you can do nothing (John15). Paul writes that we can do all things through Christ who gives us strength (Philippians 4:13). Heavyweight boxer Evander Holyfield defeated the invincible undefeated Mike Tyson at the time because he put his faith in God. David defeated Goliath because he trusted God. It is vitally important men and extremely necessary for you to build and to strengthen your relationship with God through prayer and through His Word. We cannot "Man Up" in our own ability. No weapon against us will prosper because God gave us a promise (Isaiah 54:17). Look to God who is the author and finisher of your Faith (Hebrews 12). We can only Show Up, Step Up, Grow Up, Go Up, Push Up,

and Pull Up when God looks down on us. He said, Ask and it will be Given to us, Seek and we will Find, and to Knock and things will Open and be made available to us (Matthew 7). Seek first His Kingdom and all that you need will be added to your life (Matthew 6:33). Start looking up to God and stop looking to people for what you really need and to accomplish and to achieve all of your purposes in life.

CHAPTER 3

TRIPLE AAA (ATTENTION, AFFECTION, AFFIRMATION)

I believe that all women need the men in their lives to meet their needs for affection, attention, and affirmations. They have a natural and internal desire and need to be noticed and paid attention to, spoken into with positive and confirming words, and touched and embraced in a healthy and wholesome way. She needs to feel adored, desired, wanted, and cherished. Women need stability and security from the men in their lives. The inconsistency and indecisiveness must stop and come to an end. They need what I call Triple AAA, and I am not referring to the emergency roadside assistance company.

When our cars break down and become disabled, we call for a tow truck to pull or carry us to a repair shop. Many of the women in our lives are breaking down as well and need to be repaired, healed, and delivered from painful and traumatic experiences. These 3 A's stand for *Attention, Affection,* and *Affirmation.* The role we fulfill in the lives of our families varies and changes periodically depending on the times and the seasons we are in. Life is lived in stages and on different levels. As God calls for us to be the Priests, Providers, and Protectors for our families, and to meet their physical, emotional, mental, and spiritual needs, we can be like a tow truck and become the vehicle that can bring them into their dreams, destinations, promises, and purposes. We perform this by becoming responsible, reliable, dependable, and accountable in our actions and behaviors towards those we love and care about and are obligated to.

When my youngest daughter was born, I learned a lot from my wife about how I can help her to become a more complete, competent, and courageous girl that would eventually evolve into womanhood. Most girls adore, admire, and strongly respect and accept their fathers' advice, counsel, wisdom, and insight through their own experience as men and how us men overall think, act, and operate. I try to be as transparent as possible with my wife and daughter about my past, present, and future ambitions. They should not have to guess or try to figure out who we really are deep down inside beneath the surface of our outward appearance.

With my sons, as boys, naturally I do not believe males need attention, affection, and affirmations to make them into better men. Men mainly focus on facts and the physical necessities of life. I always say men need primarily two main things: #1 Respect (Honor) and #2 Sex (Physical Satisfaction). This is why we need God's help to be sensitive and concerned about the emotional well-being of the females within our lives. I have witnessed through the lives of my sisters and my wife, who all grew up without a healthy relationship with their fathers or even significant other men in their lives as boyfriends and husbands, and even as a Pastor I have observed the horrible and devastating destructive lifestyles that are developed as a result of deficiencies in these areas for women. The absence of a father's or husband's efforts in meeting the needs of the ladies in their lives, allows for many broken and dysfunctional hearts, insurmountable anger, and unforgiveness that so many women possess, and an unstable and irrational mindset that describes and labels so many of our hurting and damaged women.

We can show ourselves to be men by changing this cultural negative circumstance. You have the opportunity to impact your daughters' and wives' lives by what you do and say on a regular basis. Before her first boyfriend, I would give my daughter cards and candy for Valentines Day to let her know how beautiful, valuable, and important she is to me as her father. I still give her healthy hugs and kisses on the cheek when we encounter each other. And I make sure to engage her in small conversations and chats to simply keep the lines of communications open and ongoing. Her confidence in who she is as a female is not based on outward opinions. It starts at home first. Her identity in knowing that she is an asset and not a liability, that she adds value to any and every environment that she is a part of, and that God and God alone validates her as a complete, competent, courageous, and whole woman. No man can now come into her life and take advantage of her weaknesses and vulnerabilities, because she is content in who she is in God. God gives us the chance to increase their chances of a happy, joy filled, and successful and victorious life.

1. Women Love and need Emotional Affection. Most women love romance and need intimacy, hugs, and tender touches. They crave gentleness, tenderness, warmth, devotion, endearment, where they feel cared for. They have a natural desire and needs that should be fulfilled by the men in their lives. Far too many of our wives and daughters are walking around vulnerable with these voids that need to be satisfied by us men. Many women, out of desperation and desire, have regrettably giving their love, heart, trust, and even resources over to undeserving men who observed and took advantage of their broken hearts, unhealthy state of mind, and their many unmet needs and desires. We have an obligation to protect, cover, and meet the female internal wants and desires. Brothers take the time and make the time to minister to the needs of the women in your life.

In marriage, we must learn how to become more intimate and romantic – contrary to what many of us were taught not to do. We were called hen-pecked men, ball and chain homebodies, soft, weak, and controlled. Yet, as we look at the many divorces, failed marriages (separated but not officially and legally), and all of the broken and dysfunctional households, we need to start doing something differently to get different results. Touching our wives non-sexually, holding hands while walking together, spontaneous hugs, and unexpected neck, shoulder, and back massages make them feel complete and gives them a desire to do even more for us and the family. The endless sacrifices that our women make daily to make sure that everyone else has their needs met, while her life remains deficient, absent, and void of what she wants and needs to make her feel complete and appreciated. They pour in so much into others, but yet struggle to be poured back into, which leads to many women feeling depleted and discouraged. I remember telling my wife when we first started dating how I do not hold hands and I do not believe in hugging. And also, how I do not cook. I was taught that makes me soft and weak and not in control. Wow how have we been lied to about what real manhood really is and more importantly, what it is not.

Meeting the physical, emotional, mental, and spiritual needs of the women in our lives is a real picture of strength, smarts, and sensitivity. I have now been married for over 27 years because I put away my ego and my pride, and I finally accepted my priorities as the "Man" of the house and the

"Leader" of my family. I help around the house with cleaning, ironing, maintenance, and I also do the outside landscaping, mowing the grass, shoveling and using the snowblower to clear our walkways, and keeping the cars repaired and occasionally grocery shopping and going to the malls and other merchants. I still have my "Mancave" time of football, basketball, boxing, and other sports, but I balance it with movies, TV shows, and other programs that my wife is interested in. Family is first. Make them a priority. Show yourself a man by making them feel appreciated and valued. Be balanced and bold!

2. Women Love and Need Endless Attention.
They spend so much time attending to details put into their hair, makeup, clothing, and appearance. Image is everything to most women. They have a strong desire to be beautiful, pretty, and attractive. They want to be wanted! We have an obligation to them to pay attention to their many adjustments and attributes attempting to keep the relationship exciting and not boring or routine. Look and compliment her as often as you can whether it's major or minor changes in their lives, such as hairstyles, perfumes and body

41

fragrances, and physical appearances as they diet and exercise. Women need to feel attractive to you men so they will eliminate the temptation to get attention from the wrong people (If you don't pay attention to her someone else will!). Flirt with her, feel on her, keep falling in love with her, and cherish and honor her. You have the capacity to remove all deficiencies, voids, and feelings of emotional emptiness that comes from the lack of attention she is not getting from who she deeply wants it to come from – her man!

So many men are ignorant and clueless when it comes to the women in their life's need for attention. They will diet, join a gym, dress a certain way, talk a particular tone, walk a certain way, and even play with you to get that much needed attention and time from you. I met my wife in a bar called the Vanity Club in Newark, N.J. I saw her when she first came into the establishment, and I was instantly and immediately attracted to her by her looks alone and how she carried herself. My infatuation and attraction to her is still strong and healthy today because she keeps herself up and together to eliminate the wrong temptations and ungodly open doors and opportunities that causes division and separation that will try to come my way.

Think back and remember how the woman in your life got your attention. What is it about her that caught your eye? How was she dressed? What fragrance was she smelling like? What was her tone of voice and her speech like? What were the unspoken vibes that drew you towards her and made you pursue her to get to know more about her? This was probably and intentionally done on her thought process in how she outwardly looked before leaving home that day. This is a true indication on how most women need and want attention and will go above and beyond with extreme measures to get it. Show yourself to be her one and only "Man" by showering and overwhelming her with undivided and undistracted attention from you. Watch and observe her positive demeanor and attitude as a result of your changed choices and commitment. Note: If by chance you are in a situation where she has let herself go and do not put as much effort into looking her best for you most of the time, ask God for ways and strategies to restore the relationship. Also make sure you are keeping your appearance correct as well. God can and will restore what's been missing and begin to fix and repair those things that produced the lack of effort on both of your parts.

3. Women Long for and Need Affirmation. Compliments, flattery, and words of encouragement mean a great deal to most women and is crucial to effective and long-lasting relationships. Most women are mainly impressed by what they "hear," unlike most men who are mainly driven by what they "see." Words and what is said in a woman's ear gate (good or bad) goes far and beyond the time that it is said. Watch your words men because once it's spoken it's hard for her to unhear and to forgive what you said. Even during arguments and heated interactions, try your best not to say something that you will regret later. She needs you to speak into her life and over her life words of empowerment, enrichment, and edification. This is so challenging for so many men who commonly have trouble communicating and talking about how they really feel about the women in their lives. Many, such as myself, have been taught that showing our real emotions makes us look weak, soft, passive, and not in control. Many men have difficulty expressing themselves through words and cannot articulate and communicate what and how they really feel inside. This makes it hard for us to give and to show affection, but we must try. We have the results of many failed marriages and relationships, and much loneliness and sorrow because of this breach between men and women. Men, listen to God's voice only, and obey Him when He convicts your heart to change what you are doing and to alter your attitude and anger.

I recall and remember putting my wife in tears and causing her to cry with my cold and inconsiderate words, and God corrected me by reminding me that she was His daughter who I was treating so badly. I got convicted and started to change my ways. Words are powerful, and they can be constructive or destructive. Use your words wisely to speak strength, security, stability, and soundness over the women whom God has entrusted you to cover. We win with words because life and death is in the power of our tongue. Tell her and tell her often how beautiful she is. How her intellect, knowledge and wisdom have enhanced and enriched the relationship and the family. If you have children, tell her how much you appreciate how she nurtures, cultivates, and raises the kids with positive qualities and principles. On special occasions, such as birthdays, Mother's Day, Christmas, Valentines

Day, and anniversaries, use cards, letters, notes, texts, emails, and voicemails to express affirmations of appreciation. The women in our lives' self-esteem, self-image, and self-value will increase and grow even stronger when we as men affirm and constantly speak strength, empowerment, and encouragement into their lives. Words of affirmation are words that communicate your love, appreciation, and respect for another person. They are positive words and phrases used to uplift someone. Affirmations have the ability to turn negative thoughts into positive and productive thoughts, and as a man or women thinketh in his or her heart so is he or she in reality.

When we begin to apply the "Triple AAA" (Attention Affection Affirmation) principles in advance, the need for lifelong therapy later will be decreased and even eliminated. It is vitally important for us men to take control over circumstances that are continually attempting to control us. Become proactive and preventative with the females in your life to guard and to protect their wellbeing. When you see the "red flags" and warning signs that your relationships are failing and headed in the wrong direction, reroute your direction by asking questions and getting outside help. Throughout our almost 30 years of being together, my wife has often conveyed and communicated to me what her and our daughters' need as it relates to how my words and my actions impact their lives tremendously whether good or bad. Staying blind to, ignorant of, and naïve to the things that are breaking families apart should no longer be tolerated by us on our "Watch!"

An amazing example of this Triple AAA principle of Affection, Attention, and Affirmation in a working relationship is found in The Book of Esther in the Bible. Mordecai, who was not Esther's biological father, demonstrated affection when her parents died and he cared for her well-being. He showed her attention in a fatherly way that nurtured her self-esteem and identity as a beautiful woman, and finally, he showed his impact in her life by affirmation, advising and counseling her to fulfill her purpose as Queen to save the Jewish people from destruction.

We also can help the women in our lives to become the Queens and Princesses that they were born to become from a spiritual standpoint, and to fulfill their purposes in life when we meet their needs for affection, attention and affirmation.

CHAPTER 4

FATHERS WE NEED YOU

Have I not spoken; shall I not bring it to pass?

Where Are the fathers? Adam where art thou? Absent fathers do a great deal of long-term damage to their children. Kids who grow up without a father often struggle socially, suffer mentally, stay stuck emotionally and even sometimes become sick physically. Feelings of being rejected and not being accepted by your own dad, creates and develops anger from the abandonment, low self-value, low self-worth, low self-esteem, and opens the opportunity for much drama, confusion, chaos, pain, and torment in one's life. The enormous and unlimited fears of trusting anyone, the unwillingness to commit towards any relationships, unable to become vulnerable, transparent, and intimate with other people.

90% of all homeless and runaway children are from fatherless homes. Fathers are supposed to be present to lay down the rules, disciplines, duties, and responsibilities such as chores, homework, Church attendance, and expectations and roles of the home. Fathers primary job in the home is to be the main disciplinarian. Fathers represent an "authority" through a sense of security, stability, and strength. Children growing up without dads develop low self-esteem, feelings of unworthiness, striving for perfection, and avoid conflict. 63% of youth suicides are from fatherless homes. Children from fatherless homes often suffer from depression, loneliness, anxiety, anger, low academic achievement, misbehavior, lying, stealing, crime, violent behavior, abusive behavior, even truancy. They are six times more likely to live in poverty. 80-90% of all convicts are from fatherless homes. Finally, many drug addicts and many alcoholics are negatively impacted from homes where fathers were absent. Show yourself a man fathers by building a healthy relationship with your children. Regardless of Baby Mama Drama! Fight for your family. Our place, position and posture in the family is vitally important if we want victory, success, and winning in every area of life. A "double-minded man" is unstable in all of his ways. Our experiences with failures, mistakes, misinformation, negative and bad learned behaviors, and unpreventable situations and circumstances makes us as men more than qualified to teach and train those that we love and care about how to avoid life damaging decisions and events.

In sports, they emphasis the importance of being in the right position at the right time to make the right plays. They practice strategy, timing, and execution to maximize their chances for defeating the opponents. Also, with cars we occasionally go to our local mechanic shops for convenience and quick minor repair and maintenance jobs. But when it comes to major auto repairs, we are forced to go back to the maker and manufacturer of the car because they designed it with particular parts and to operate a specific way. God has designed the family structure a specific way to work with the parents and the children. We as men must begin to do things God's way to remove the division, discord, dysfunction, and death of so many broken families.

Far too often, our daughters spend a lot of wasted time and years looking for love in all of the wrong places and with the wrong men. While our sons sometimes struggle with their identity as men and with not knowing how to treat and handle women or children, along with developing the inability and the capacity to keep a job or to succeed in a substantial career. We have a responsibility like David did with Solomon, of giving directions on how to leave a lasting legacy throughout our bloodlines and to the generations that will follow. Fathers, provoke your children not to anger but raise them in the fear and admonition of the Lord. I have always lived my life as a guarded and skeptical person because I was angry with my father for abandoning me, and I never cared for confusion and drama too much. I come to realize now that it was always a trust issue where I did not want to be hurt, manipulated, or taken advantage of by anyone to the degree that I was hurt, wounded, and disappointed by my father. My father's absence from my life really created in me a distrust towards people. I discovered later in my life that avoidance is not the answer or solution – it sometimes makes matters even worse. I was attempting to run away and to stay away from hurt and trauma at all costs, by avoiding being vulnerable to anyone, and by being in control of my connections and network. To repent means to reroute. We cannot continue to live in denial of our own failures and shortcomings as men. Face it to fix it. It's not how we start but it's how we finish that matters the most. A bad beginning does not have to have a bad ending.

Most men naturally have a competitive nature and love to compete and compare themselves to others. But God says, I know the thoughts I think towards you, thoughts of good things and not bad things, thoughts of you having a great future and expected success in every area of life (Jerimiah 29:11). Cain saw his brother Abel as competition for God's approval and acceptance. He became envious, jealous, and angry over God receiving Abel's offering and rejecting Cain's offering (Genesis 4). Men who have been rejected and neglected develop anger issues, and many become hostile and abusive. And until they are healed and made whole through the Word of God, they leave a trail of hurting, abused, confused, and dysfunctional people that they are responsible for. The first murder and shedding of blood was recorded as a result of Cain not willing to change. God said to him to do good and good will come back to you, but instead, he killed his brother in rage and brought a curse upon his life.

God, knowing all things, asked Cain about the whereabouts of his brother Abel, and Cain had the audacity to ask God a foolish question, "Am I my brother's keeper?"

God responds by telling Cain, I know exactly where your brother is because his shed blood is speaking to me from the ground.

Brothers, we must begin to hold each other accountable. Stop competing and comparing yourself with others but begin to compete with yourself by becoming better every single day. God is the ultimate judge of our actions and behaviors. When I was running the streets as a married man in my first marriage, I wish somebody would have had the courage to teach me right from wrong, but instead, they encouraged my ungodly actions all the more. Without conviction, there will be no change! We need more men like David to learn from their own personal mistakes and bad decisions and talk to us about the many negative consequences that come from unrighteous living.

We fight not against flesh and blood, but against evil and unclean spirits (Ephesians 6). The weapons of our warfare are not carnal, but they are mighty to pull down strongholds and to remove barriers that block or interfere with our blessings. I had a big struggle relating to my sons and even to my four biological brothers because of the hurt and wounds that my absent father left me with. If you are a man and grew up without a good godly example of a father like King Solomon had with David, chances are you have had many struggles in your family, personal, and even business relationships. That is why I believe God wanted me to share my transformation experience from being a broken and dysfunctional man into a whole and healed and happy and holy husband, father, son, and financially stable man of God. In a world filled with so many temptations, distractions, disruptions, delays, drama, disappointments, discouragement, and warfare, you must implement three principles into your life as you become the developed and disciplined disciple of Christ and the emerging leader of your family as head of your household. Like Joshua you will someday make the declaration with confidence that as for you and your house, you will serve the Lord. 1. Become a man of Prayer. 2. Become a man of Praise 3. Become a man of Patience. David and Solomon practiced and did all three of these principles on a regular basis. Remember the story of the Amalekites taking David's wives and children, and his men wanted to stone him to death, but David prayed and encouraged himself in the Lord, and asked God in prayer with the Ephod (priestly spiritual garment) on, although he was not a Priest, and God told him to pursue the enemy and take his family back, and he recovered all that was taken and lost. You also, when you pray, God will show you what you need to do and change about your life to show yourself a man. Solomon prayed and asked God for wisdom, and God granted wisdom that was superior to any other human being who ever lived, and God also gave him what he did not pray for as a bonus, such as long life, wealth and health, and power and victory over all of his enemies. You also, after you pray to God, will receive wisdom and knowledge that will give you answers to all of your problems, and grace and mercy against all of your enemies and haters (Psalm 34).

David said, "I will bless the Lord at all times and his Praise will always be in my mouth. David danced and praised God with all his might when they recovered the Ark of God. Men, when we praise God and give Him thanks always, God rewards us with prosperity and protection. Solomon praised God after the completion of building the temple, and the glory of God showed up. When you praise God, it is not a sign of weakness, but it is a sign of strength, and God's glory will shine upon your life. King Jehosaphat prayed and praised, and God gave him victory over his enemies. Paul and Silas prayed and praised, and God set them free from bondage. Prayer and praise are spiritual weapons for spiritual warfare. That is an evil and wicked spirit that's coming against you and your family.

David, while hiding in the Cave of Adullam from his enemies had to demonstrate patience and wait until God began to send him help. Solomon had to demonstrate patience because his brothers wrongfully tried to take his throne. You must learn and understand that God has a set time for you to be totally delivered and healed. Help is on the way my brother, but wait for it and don't get in a hurry. Solomon waited for David's people to receive him as their king because he had to first prove to them that he could become a great leader. That is God's desire for you sir, to become a great leader in your family and in your community. David had a lot of sons who disqualified themselves from the throne by disobeying God and performing evil against their father David. Absalom had a controlling and take-over spirit, and tried to overthrow David's authority by force, and it eventually caused him to lose his life. Adonijah, as David is about to die, takes it upon himself to become David's successor, and rallied some of his father's loyal leaders to rebel against David and make Adonijah their new king. Yet David's wife Bathsheba, the Prophet Nathan who David honored and respected and the Captain of David's army, came and reminded David of God's decision to make Solomon the King after his death.

See brothers, what God has for you, is for you, and nothing or no one can change that. So do your absolute best to stay in the will of God. That Jezebel and Delilah spirit that stopped Ahab and Sampson from fulfilling their destiny, is still alive and active trying to temp and trap us as well. I will never forget my battle against stage 2 colon cancer. It was a 2-year process filled with setbacks, pain, problems, and fear. Yet because I applied these three principles of Prayer, Praise, and Patience, I celebrate and praise God every day of my life for giving me victory over cancer. God will also give you Victory if you put your faith and Trust in Him. My blended family did not blend and mix well right away, but with much prayer, praise, and patience we are now whole, working, and worshipping God as a united family of harmony.

There is a process and preparation period for you to become a man pleasing to God. I truly can relate to living under a cursed life. Up until age 30 when I totally and fully released my life over to God, so many bad and horrible and traumatic events devastated me and stole away so many of my God given opportunities towards a better and more fulfilled life. Since making that decision to submit and surrender my life to God, I have experienced so much more success in my family, finances, and friendships. God has recompensed me with restoration, recovery, and rewards as I began to live by faith in His Word in the Bible.

As I reflect on the conversations between David and his son, I still get sad and even angry because I, like so many men, never had a conversation, talk, experience of any kind with my own biological father. David knew God from firsthand experience as a protector, provider, and promise keeper. Can you imagine the one that killed a lion and a bear, the one who killed the giant Goliath, the one who when they almost stoned him didn't break, but he encouraged himself, and yes, the one who had to repent for killing Uriah and numbering the people, is now advising his son on how to rule and reign with a spirit of excellence.

Ask yourself a serious question and try to be as honest as you can be... Are you in the perfect or permissive will of God? Your life will become so fruitful and productive if you be willing and obedient to the Word of God (Isaiah 1). God comes to Abraham in the book of Genesis and says to him, leave your family and this familiar environment and go to a place of prosperity that I will show you. And I will bless those that bless you and I will curse those that curse you. And all the families in the Earth will be blessed because of your decision. The God of Abraham, Isaac, and Jacob generational blessings and promises happened because they obeyed God with the wisdom and advice from their forefathers and the previous generations.

When Jesus shed His Blood on the cross for the forgiveness of mankind's sins which could not be erased any other way except for this perfect sacrifice of the Son of God – the Lamb of God, He died that we all might have a chance to live a life of abundance. He said the Thief comes to steal, kill, and destroy but He came for us to have an opportunity for a better quality of life. The only way we really can become the men that God created us to be is to live and follow the example of how Jesus conducted himself, behavior, prayed, and interactions with other people. He said if you want to be my disciple, there are three things you must do.

1. Deny yourself. Remove pride and humble yourself by walking in humility and remain teachable and not arrogant. Also sacrifice some fun, pleasure, time, money, energy, and wants for the Kingdom's sake. Peter said, we left everything to follow you and Jesus replied, you will get it all back and much more from me for the effort.

2. Take up your cross. The pain and problems of life are the process and preparation that God uses to counter the devil's plan for our demise and destruction. He uses our weaknesses like lust, pride, greed, anger, and ignorance of God's Word, against us to separate us from God and cause all kinds of division and dysfunction in our families.

3. Follow me. Jesus has given us an example of how to conduct ourselves and walk in integrity and success when it comes to our families, our careers, and everything else related to life.

We are called to become the Priest, Provider, and Protector of our families. As priest, we serve as the spiritual leader that prays and covers our wives and children, as provider, the man who works and hustles and does whatever it takes that's legal to earn wages to keep a roof over his family's head, food on the table, and meet all necessary needs such as medical, dental, vision, and other benefits. The Bible says a man who does not work is worse than an infidel or unbeliever. What a strong and wakeup call statement for many men who have been raised and babied by mothers who do not know how to train boys into responsible men. As protectors, we must be physically present to handle and to deal with anyone or anything trying to violate or manipulate those who you love and care about compassionately. We are obligated to watch over our loved ones by any means necessary. Let him who steals, steal no more. My father did not protect and cover us as a family, and as a result drug addictions, abuse, alcoholism, poverty, pain, and problems came in and destroyed so many of my siblings' dreams, aspirations, and yes even their lives prematurely. Men our very presence in the family structure that God created represents stability, strength, security, and safety. When women and children see a man around, it gives them a firm foundation to rely on. When my daughters have car or relationship problems that come unexpectedly, they can call on me to show up and to stabilize the negative situation with my wisdom, guidance, and personal experiences. Even my wife occasionally will have an emotional response or reaction to a serious situation, but I will attempt to logically and practically react not in my feelings or emotions but in stability of mind. You have the potential also to settle things down that arise out of nowhere. We also bring our physical and natural strength to the table. Men are naturally designed by God to be stronger than women. Heavy lifting of furniture or outdoor tasks, bringing groceries into the house, or taking out the garbage, repairs around the house that requires a strong hand, and even humorously when a dog or wild animal seems threatening, we use our strength to handle it.

Spiritual covering, protection and provision are all necessary and important when it comes to a man's position in the family. As I am writing this book, I have been working for FedEx for over 37 years. It has been a great honor for me to take care of my family financially and supply them with medical benefits, vision and dental insurance, car and life insurance, and all other needs that require money. Men, we must work and hustle legally to financially bring security into our family environment.

Finally, we represent safety for the family. Everyone seems to feel safer when a man is involved. They feel protected and valued when we make the time to be there for them. We are the "spiritual shelter" in times of storms and trouble that periodically appear and that randomly show up from time to time.

CHAPTER 5

CHANGE THE WAY YOU THINK

A nother way we as men show ourselves to be a man is by putting on the mind of Christ. He made a powerful declaration and statement when His parents Mary and Joseph was frantically looking for Him after losing touch with Him for three days. They finally found Him in the synagogue talking with and teaching the priests and religious rulers. As they discussed with Him how worried they were about Him being alone in a strange place at 12 years old, He stated and explained to them how He must be about His father's business.

We as men should develop that same sense of urgency as it relates to the Kingdom of God and converting souls for Christ. God wishes that no one would perish but that all would repent. We need role models, mentors, and coaches to replace so many absent fathers if we are going to fulfill the prophecy of Malachi to turn the hearts of the fathers back to their sons, and the sons' hearts back towards their fathers. I am so grateful and thankful for my sons forgiving me for some of my wrongs and bad choices over the years, and we now enjoy respectful and rewarding relationships with each other. I have talked to many men whose kids want nothing to do with them and are not even on speaking terms. It breaks my heart when I hear those stories because I know the importance of the role of a father in their child's life. A family divided cannot stand. I have seen this work out in my own life as I now have a good relationship with my sons.

Whether we had good godly examples and advice or not, we have a second chance by grace and mercy to reverse the curse. Even with fathers that were there and responsible and showed some of us how to be a man, we need the anointing to destroy the yokes of the devil against men. The spirit is willing, but the body is weak. So many men are led and controlled by their lust than by being led by the Lord Jesus. Even Solomon, the wisest king to ever live, had weaknesses. His love for idolatrous women destroyed his legacy of a man on the throne. He was not considered an evil king like some, but yet his lust for women and to please them in spite of God's commands, made God to come against his reign and opportunity.

I was so fortunate and blessed to come up in a Church that had a strong and intentional emphasis on helping men in their struggles and shortcomings. Man to Man Bible Study, accountability groups, Khalfani Big Brother mentoring groups, and even Men's Prayer Groups and Men's Retreats and Conferences were paramount in my development as a man because of the teaching and sharing – keeping it real, candid, and sometimes painful and hurtful memories of boyhood that so many men do not know how to address or fix. If we lack wisdom God says ask Him and He will give it to us. David in Psalm 51 repents and asks God to forgive him for killing Uriah, sleeping with his wife, and impregnating her with a baby born in sin that eventually died. Nathan the Prophet was sent to David by God to rebuke him for his actions, and conviction of the heart allowed David to see his wrong against this family and against God. He asked God to renew his spirit and to create in him a clean heart.

I remember the years I spent having a dirty, unclean, ungodly, and evil heart. I was very angry over so many things. Seeing my mother struggle

SHOW YOURSELF A MAN

to pay bills and raise eight kids by herself. Witnessing my two sisters as they struggled with alcoholism and drug addiction and eventually die prematurely also because of an absent father that did not give them the attention, affection, and affirmation that every woman needs and longs for. I was angry with my ex-wife that did hurtful and distrustful things towards me as I also did towards her. Angry about losing my first-born daughter at only 6 days of age to a rare congenital heart disease. Angry about being fired from jobs unjustly. And simply angry with myself for making so many mistakes and foolish dumb decisions over the course of my life.

Many men are so angry today and they do not know how to process that anger. The Bible says be slow to anger, slow to speak, and quick to listen and let not the sun go down on your wrath. Yet many men go to bed angry and wake up angry and it's a lifelong, destructive cycle. They become criminals as a result and spend years in and out of prison. Some become addicted to drugs and alcohol, and even abusive to their wives, girlfriends, and children (narcissists) because they feel powerless and useless. Some even become reckless and dangerous to themselves and others with the way they drive, eat, behave, and are not responsible with what God has blessed them with including family, finances, and friendships.

If you save a man by way of salvation, you have the chance to save an entire family and generation because there is something so compelling and unique about the authority that God has giving us as men. As a man thinketh in his heart so is he. Change the way you think. Renew your mind if you learned to do life the wrong way or the world's way. Your disciplines will determine your destiny, not just your desires. Consistency is the key to maturity and success in every area of life. Practice makes perfect. We have to train ourselves as men to do life according to God's ways. Pride will not allow that, only humility – saying, God I need your help. Paul said there is a battle, a war, between the body and the spirit constantly. And only with the help of Christ will the spirit win. Many men want to do and become better, but they just do not know how.

I remember on so many occasions how God helped me and rescued me from trouble and negative situations. Like the time I was stopped by the police and was drinking and driving with no valid registration or car insurance, but when I went to court, I remember my mom telling me to pray and to ask God to get me out of this predicament because I could lose my job at Fed Ex. And the judge eventually ordered me to pay a small fine and to make sure I get my credentials in order. As I sat in that courtroom and saw him revoke and suspend so many people's driver's licenses, I was so thankful for him giving me this opportunity. I recall the incident that I spoke about earlier in the book where me and my friend got caught selling marijuana illegally and as they were driving us to the police precent to arrest us, they stopped the car suddenly and let us out and told us to walk back home. When I got home, I told my mother a part truth about what happened, and she said to me, "I began to pray because I knew one of my children was in trouble."

That comment from her stuck with me up until this day. That's why I strongly believe in the power of prayer and the prayer of faith. I know prayer works. My youngest son Marcus was born with an epileptic seizure disorder that challenged and came against his health and well-being as a child. His neurologist prescribed medicine that would help to manage his episodes, yet they still would occur periodically. I remember after one incident while we were visiting friends at a marriage ministry event, Marcus became unresponsive with his communication. As we were driving back home, he suddenly spoke out of nowhere and said to us that God just spoke to him and told him that he was going to be all right. We immediately were moved with shock and amazement and asked him to repeat what he just said. And without hesitation he declared once again of God reassuring him that he would be okay. He was about eight years old when that happened, yet that situation stayed with me as I wondered about how amazing and awesome our God is. – To speak directly to our children about their future and destiny! It still moves me of how God really cares about us as individuals. My wife and I have prayed for his healing for many years and as a result, he is now totally healed of seizures and no longer has to take medicine for that.

I thank God for allowing me to become the dad that I never had. The Bible says train up a child in the way they should go, and they will not depart from it. I have tried to be a good father figure and an example of the head of household in covering my family and providing for their physical, emotional, mental, and spiritual needs. David, unlike his father Jesse, did not overlook the needs and voids in his son Solomon's life. He knew what it felt like not to be considered to be a man of value and purpose. When God sent the Prophet Samuel to Jesse's house to anoint the next king of Israel, his father did not even consider David to be a qualified candidate. But God said to Samuel that people are so impressed with outward appearances and gifts, but God judges our hearts.

David was a man that really wanted to please God more than anything else. My prayer for you as a reader of this material and principles, is that you to would be or become a strong man seeking God and discovering His will and purpose for your life. So many men struggle with a prideful and hard heart that will not humble themselves enough for God to teach them what they need to do to change for the better.

Choice, Change, and Commitment are the principles I live by. I call these the 3 C's to success in any and every area of life. First, there's choice. A man who is decisive and discerning is a powerful man. A doubleminded man, the Word declares, will be unstable, shaky, and vulnerable to fail and fall at any given moment. Ask God in unwavering faith for answers and wisdom. We all are faced with the same temptations, distractions, and drama that are in our complicated world today. God alerted us from the beginning of creation that life would be full of choices and decisions. Starting in the Garden of Eden after creating man in His own image and likeness, God gave man free will to choose knowing full well that many of us will naturally choose wrong over right. He told Adam, you can eat from all of the trees in the garden but do not eat from the one tree known for good and knowledge.

Adam disobeyed God and ate from the one tree that was forbidden and allowed sin to gain access into his life. The wages of sin produces death and destruction. Sin comes to stop, block, and to prevent us from receiving God's best. But when we choose God over the things of the world, we begin to win at life and to get victory over all of our battles and struggles.

Secondly, change on the other hand, is very hard but very necessary. How we take care of ourselves by eating right and exercising. How we treat and conduct ourselves whether personal or business. Thirdly, how we develop and secure our relationship with God. Most men do not put forth the effort and energy to change negative behaviors because it sometimes seems impossible to fix just how dysfunctional and broken we are as men. But when we go to God with a sincere and genuine heart asking Him to help us, and when we are really transparent and real and honest about our struggles, He will give us transforming power to change.

The thief, our enemy the devil, is hoping that our faith will fail and as a result we will fulfill sometimes self-created failures and losses. Far too many men spend their entire lives feeling like failures and unqualified and useless. The enemy attacks us through negative thoughts that teach us such. But the Bible says we are to take every thought captive and make it obedient to Christ's ways. His thoughts are higher than our thoughts and His ways are higher than our ways. As a man thinketh in his heart so is he. We must shift negative mindsets into positive mindsets. Remember, no conviction, no change. It's not how we start but how we finish that counts. In sports, there are record breaking comebacks in every sport, because if you don't quit and give up on yourself, you will recover all. A setback is a setup for a comeback.

Sometimes we, like Jacob, have to wrestle with God and not let go until He blesses us. Jacob so desperately wanted to change from being a liar and a deceiver, into becoming a strong man of God that he was willing to wrestle with God and not let go until God changed him. You must also develop this kind of determination to become the best version of yourself possible.

There are many proven patterns and principles that will produce fruit in your life. As a man coming into the family of God from the world, God began to change my character. I was angry, a liar and deceiver, lustful and prideful, unforgiving, and sinful and sin filled. So I said yes to His process of transforming my life. I was failing as a father, husband, and provider and protector. So He equipped me with anointed men who had greater wisdom and experience than I did. I was given access to things and events such as Man to Man Bible Studies where I witnessed men being set free from bad bondages such as addictions to drugs and alcohol, abusive behaviors, pornography, pride, and anger. I regularly went on men's retreats where we were taught about how to train our ungodly traits and characteristics into positive and helpful ones. I learned and discovered how important and paramount it is to have accountability partners that would pray over my weaknesses and ignorance in certain areas. I was encouraged to read a lot of books on marriage, parenting, Christianity, family, and financial security. Strongholds and familiar spirits are used by the enemy to keep us in bondage and stuck in suffering and sickness. But Jesus said that the Spirit of the Lord was upon Him and anointed Him to open up the eyes of the blind, to heal the brokenhearted, to set the captives free, and to release new opportunities of good from God.

I was in the dark, I was broken, I was stuck, and I was producing more bad than good. But my faith in Jesus and His power to change me and to change my reality made all the difference in the world.

Finally, through commitment, I can confidently say now that I am showing myself a man by demonstrating disciplines that are constructive and not destructive. I am committed to being priest, provider, and protector for my family. I am committed to being the man and the leader that God has created me to be. I am committed to fulfilling my assignment here on Earth. Now I have a question for you. Are you committed?

Create a Christian culture in your home that consists of prayer, devotions, fellowship, and songs. An atmosphere of praise to God that will become an environment for miracles, breakthroughs, and blessings. God will show up in your life and in your home. God will continually equip you to be the man, the leader, the priest, provider, and protector that He created you to be.

God will open doors for you and provide opportunities for you to show yourself a man wherever you go and in all that you do!

I'll close with this scripture:

What is man that you are mindful of him?
And the son of man that You visit him?
For you have made him a little lower than the
angels.
And you have crowned him with glory and honor.
You have made him to have dominion over the
works of Your hands.
You have put all things under his feet,
All sheep and oxen—Even the beasts of the field,
The birds of the air; And the fish of the sea
That pass through the paths of the seas.
O LORD, our Lord,
How excellent is Your name in all the earth!
Psalm 8:4-9

ABOUT THE AUTHOR

Anthony Simmons, also known lovingly as Pastor Anthony, was born and raised in Newark, New Jersey. After graduating at the top ten of his class, he attended Fairleigh Dickinson University, where he majored in engineering. He also attended University of Phoenix with a major in Business.

He pastors New Creation Christian Ministries, which prior to the pandemic, was located in Hillside, New Jersey for 7 years and before that, the church was located in Elizabeth, New Jersey for 7 years. Currently the ministry is set up virtually to reach the masses as he and his wife, take the Gospel global and preach the Word to the world. He is a prophetic preacher and a profound teacher who God is using to manifest His Kingdom in the lives of those under his covering. He has traveled around the United States to speak at conferences, summits, seminars, and other events. He is a powerful prolific speaker who enjoys motivating, educating, and inspiring others.

He is also currently employed with FEDEX One where He has worked for the past 37 years.

He has been married to Dr. Rebecca Simmons for the past 28 years. He is the father of four children, grandfather of four, and great grandfather of one.

He is a man of integrity, character, and great faith. He is a phenomenal leader in his family, church, and community. He is the author of *Making Marriage and Relationships Work,* which he cowrote with his wife, and *Victory Over Cancer, Winning Every Battle In Life,* which tells of his journey through receiving and walking through the healing process of a cancer diagnosis.

He is a powerful speaker who is being used to transform minds and positively impact lives.

ORDER INFORMATION

You can order additional copies of *Show Yourself A Man* by using the email address below.

Anthony Simmons

Email Address: showyourselfaman@gmail.com

Books are available at Amazon.com,
Kindle and Your Local Bookstores (By Request)

Please leave a review for this book on Amazon and let other readers know how much you enjoyed reading it.

Thank you!

www.ingramcontent.com/pod-product-compliance
Lightning Source LLC
Chambersburg PA
CBHW052209090426
42741CB00010B/2464